British English

Caroline Nixon &
Michael Tomlinson

Activity Book

with Digital Pack

1

Thanks and Acknowledgements

Many thanks to everyone at Cambridge University Press and Assessment for their dedication and hard work, and in particular to:

Liane Grainger and Lynn Townsend for supervising the whole project and guiding us calmly through the storms;

Alison Bewsher for her keen editorial eye, enthusiasm and great suggestions;

Zara Hutchinson-Goncalves for her energy, enthusiasm and helpful suggestions.

We would also like to thank all our pupils and colleagues, past, present and future, at Star English academy in Murcia, especially Jim Kelly for his friendship and support throughout the years.

This is for Lydia and Silvia, my own 'Stars', with all my love. – CN

For Paloma, for her love, encouragement and unwavering support. Thanks. MT

The authors and publishers acknowledge the following sources of copyright material and are grateful for the permissions granted. While every effort has been made, it has not always been possible to identify the sources of all the material used, or to trace all copyright holders. If any omissions are brought to our notice, we will be happy to include the appropriate acknowledgements on reprinting and in the next update to the digital edition, as applicable.

Key: R= Review, U = Unit

Photography

The following photos are sourced from Getty Images.

U1: romrodinka/iStock/Getty Images Plus; ViewStock; JGI/Jamie Grill; radnatt/RooM; Granger Wootz; Khosrork/iStock/Getty Images Plus; SchulteProductions/Photographer's Choice RF; **U2:** IlexImage/E+; skodonnell/iStock/Getty Images Plus; Coprid/iStock/Getty Images Plus; Anatoliy Sadovskiy/iStock/Getty Images Plus; deepblue4you/E+; Ko Hong-Wei/EyeEm; koosen/iStock/Getty Images Plus; Nichcha Sombutpanich/EyeEm; **U3:** broeb/iStock/Getty Images Plus; Yasser Chalid/Moment; pioneer111/iStock/Getty Images Plus; Nirut Sangkeaw/EyeEm; sweetym/E+; boitano/iStock/Getty Images Plus; malerapaso/E+; Puripat1981/iStock/Getty Images Plus; gldburger/iStock; underworld111/iStock/Getty Images Plus; John Lamb/The Image Bank; pekour/iStock/Getty Images Plus; **U4:** FlairImages/iStock/Getty Images Plus; Jose Luis Pelaez Inc/DigitalVision; Daniel Tardif/DigitalVision; fizkes/iStock/Getty Images Plus; SDI Productions/E+; Inti St Clair; twinsterphoto/iStock/Getty Images Plus; dszc/E+; 4x6/iStock/Getty Images Plus; Halfpoint/iStock/Getty Images Plus; kate_sept2004/E+; Juanmonino/iStock/Getty Images Plus; mdphoto16/E+; DjelicS/E+; Alejandra de la Fuente/Moment; Oliver Rossi/Stone; Image Source; Devi Sankar/EyeEm; Zach Krings/EyeEm; Philippe LEJEANVRE/Moment; Gary Mayes/Moment; Phillip Gatward/Cultura; fstop123/E+; HRAUN/E+; Silke Klewitz-Seemann; bymuratdeniz/iStock/Getty Images Plus; malerapaso/E+; AlexanderFord/E+; ajr_images/iStock/Getty Images Plus; John Rensten/The Image Bank; Morsa Images/DigitalVision; Kelvin Murray/Photodisc; Poike/iStock/Getty Images Plus; PT Images; Richard Newstead/Moment; RossiAgung/iStock/Getty Images Plus; Dimitri Otis/Stone; Images say more about me than words./Moment; Adastra/The Image Bank; Tokarsky/iStock/Getty Images Plus; Antonio M. Rosario/The Image Bank; buradaki/iStock/Getty Images Plus; Science Photo Library - SCIEPRO/Brand X Pictures; FatCamera/iStock/Getty Images Plus; Ariel Skelley/Photodisc; Mieke Dalle/Photographer's Choice/Getty Images Plus; **R1–4:** koosen/iStock/Getty Images Plus; malerapaso/E+; Puripat1981/iStock/Getty Images Plus; Devi Sankar/EyeEm; fstop123/E+; Kelvin Murray/Photodisc; Kinson C Photography/Moment Open; skodonnell/iStock/Getty Images Plus; Puripat1981/iStock/Getty Images Plus; JoKMedia/E+; Anatoliy Sadovskiy/iStock/Getty Images Plus; John Rensten/The Image bank; Sergiy1975/iStock/Getty Images Plus; hudiemm/E+; Creative Crop/DigitalVision; Philippe LEJEANVRE/Moment; malerapaso/Moment; loveguli/E+; Marianna Lishchenco/iStock/Getty Images Plus; triloks/E+; sweetym/E+; Coprid/iStock/Getty Images Plus; Alvaro Tejero/iStock/Getty Images Plus; Zach Krings/EyeEm; **U5:** GlobalP/iStock/Getty Images Plus; MediaProduction/E+; sserg_dibrova/iStock/Getty Images Plus; axelbueckert/iStock/Getty Images Plus; cynoclub/iStock/Getty Images Plus; GlobalP/iStock/Getty Images Plus; raw/iStock/Getty Images Plus; Andregric/iStock/Getty Images Plus; Dougal Waters/DigitalVision; Parkpoom Doungkaew/EyeEm; Elles Rijsdijk/EyeEm; Algefoto/iStock/Getty Images Plus; Adrian Coleman/E+; nigelb10/iStock/Getty Images Plus; Engdao Wichitpunya/EyeEm; Péter Hegedűs/500px Prime; Georgette Douwma/Stockbyte; **U6:** strike0/iStock/Getty Images Plus; Alastair Pollock Photography/Moment; Szilvia Pap-Kutasi/500px; Roy JAMES Shakespeare/Photodisc; Westend61; bubaone/DigitalVision Vectors; Christopher Hopefitch/DigitalVision; Yellow Dog Productions/The Image Bank; simonlong/Moment; Nils Jacobi/iStock/Getty Images Plus; **U7:** Olga Kurbatova/iStock/Getty Images Plus; **U8:** simonlong/Stone; goinyk/iStock/Getty Images Plus; Matteo Colombo/Moment; Ethel Peisker Lacerda/EyeEm; elmvilla/iStock/Getty Images Plus; Patrice Hauser/The Image Bank/Getty Images Plus; David Rowland/The Image Bank/Getty Images Plus; Mark Hamblin/Oxford Scientific/Getty Images Plus; QuimGranell/Moment/Getty Images Plus; Lian van den Heever/Gallo Images/Getty Images Plus; kuritafsheen/RooM; Rafael Ben-Ari/The Image Bank/Getty Images Plus; fstop123/E+; Imgorthand/E+; Dean Mitchell/E+; Jose Luis Pelaez Inc/DigitalVision; Artyom Kozhemyakin/iStock/Getty Images Plus; **R5–8:** Georgette Douwma/Stone; ToscaWhi/iStock/Getty Images Plus; Patricia Doyle/Corbis Documentary; Sergey Ryumin/Moment; Ignacio Palacios/Stone; Darren Robb/The Image Bank; Ulli Bonnekamp/Photodisc; **U9:** StockPlanets/E+; Stockbyte; Santiago Urquijo/Moment; maccj/iStock/Getty Images Plus; Kris Timken; HRAUN/E+; Fabio Alcini/500Px Plus; simonlong/Moment; Rafa Fernández/EyeEm; ilbusca/iStock/Getty Images Plus; Tim Hawley/Photographer's Choice/Getty Images Plus; Fajrul Islam/Moment; monkeybusinessimages/iStock/Getty Images Plus; Tsuneo Yamashita/Taxi Japan/Getty Images Plus; Zero Creatives/Cultura; Stas Zakshevskiy/EyeEm; David Madison/Stone; master1305/iStock/Getty Images Plus; Gearstd/iStock/Getty Images Plus; Photodisc; Nalinratana Phiyanalinmat/EyeEm; Drazen Stader/EyeEm; Andriy Onufriyenko/Moment; Samus Henderson/EyeEm; Johner Images; SasinT Gallery/Moment; **U10:** Adamo Di Loreto/iStock/Getty Images Plus; anhoog/iStock/Getty Images Plus; phive2015/iStock/Getty Images Plus; alxpin/E+; Henglein And Steets/Photolibrary; Carl & Ann Purcell/The Image Bank Unreleased; Andrius Aleksandravicius/EyeEm; Henglein And Steets/Photolibrary; Tryaging/iStock; prospective56/iStock/Getty Images Plus; avid_creative/E+; Zia Soleil/Stone; kali9/E+; Katja Zimmermann/The Image Bank; FatCamera/E+; **U11:** Letizia Le Fur/ONOKY; Jeff Greenough; Wealan Pollard/OJO Images; vgajic/iStock/Getty Images Plus; JGI/Jamie Grill; Patricia Abecina/EyeEm; Gearstd/iStock/Getty Images Plus; 3dgoksu/E+; Eduard Lysenko/iStock/Getty Images Plus; C Squared Studios/Photodisc; kemalbas/iStock/Getty Images Plus; **U12:** MichaelJay/iStock/Getty Images Plus; Wealthylady/iStock/Getty Images Plus; vfoto/iStock/Getty Images Plus; Westend61; Ljupco/iStock/Getty Images Plus; unpict/iStock/Getty Images Plus; Nattawut Lakjit/EyeEm; tunart/E+; Voren1/iStock/Getty Images Plus; Stockbyte; popovaphoto/iStock/Getty Images Plus; robertsre/iStock/Getty Images Plus; bergamont/iStock/Getty Images Plus; Michael Burrell/iStock/Getty Images Plus; BWFolsom/iStock/Getty Images Plus; ThinkDeep/E+; carlosalvarez/iStock/Getty Images Plus; arkstart/iStock/Getty Images Plus; Thor Hakonsen/Moment Open; Martin Harvey/DigitalVision; GlobalP/iStock/Getty Images Plus; vusta/E+; gerenme/E+; Dmytro Synelnychenko/iStock/Getty Images Plus; Renaud Philippe/EyeEm; wilatlak villette/Moment; Nenov/Moment; digitalgenetics/iStock/Getty Images Plus; Wong Sze Fei/EyeEm; Antagain/E+; eli_asenova/iStock/Getty Images Plus; DNY59/E+; CasarsaGuru/iStock/Getty Images Plus; xavierarnau/E+; Jill Giardino; JanuarySkyePhotography/Moment; LindaYolanda/E+; Ross Whitaker/The Image Bank; Kelvin Murray/Phtodisc; damircudic/E+.

The following photos are sourced from other libraries.

U2: Gino Santa Maria/Shutterstock; **U11:** HeinzTeh/Shutterstock. Commissioned photography by Copy cat and Trevor Clifford Photography.

Illustrations

Pronk Media Inc.; Beth Hughes (The Bright Agency); Clara Soriano (The Bright Agency); Dan Crisp (The Bright Agency); Gaby Zemeno (Direct artist); Jake McDonald (The Bright Agency); Matthew Scott (The Bright Agency).

Cover Photography by Hulinska_Yevheniia/iStock/Getty Images Plus.

Video

Video acknowledgements are in the Teacher Resources on Cambridge One.

Audio

Audio production by Creative Listening.

Design and typeset

Blooberry Design

Additional authors

Katy Kelly: Monty's Sounds and Spelling
Rebecca Legros: Marie's art, geography and science
Montse Watkin: Exam folders

Contents

1 Hello!

1 Look and match.

2 🎧 2 Listen and circle the tick or cross.

Vocabulary: character names   ▶ Do the online activities on Practice Extra as you complete this unit.

Look, match and say.

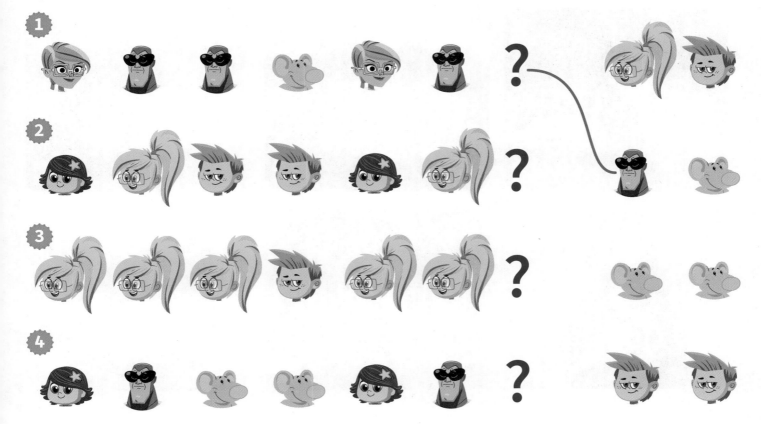

 Join the dots.

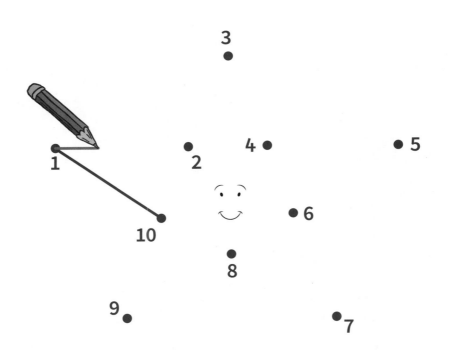

1 🎧 3 Listen and write the number.

6

2 Draw and write.

Me!

I'm _____Paula_____.
I'm _____seven_____.

Me!

I'm _____.
I'm _____.

Vocabulary: numbers 1–10

1 🎧 4 🐵 **Listen and colour.**

Monty's sounds and spelling

 Look, circle and colour.

r

2 **Write and draw.**

_ed _ainbow

My picture dictionary

1 **Find and stick.**

| one | two | three |
| four | five | six |

My star card

2 **Say the words. Colour the stars.**

2 ★ My school

1 🎧 5 **Listen and colour.**

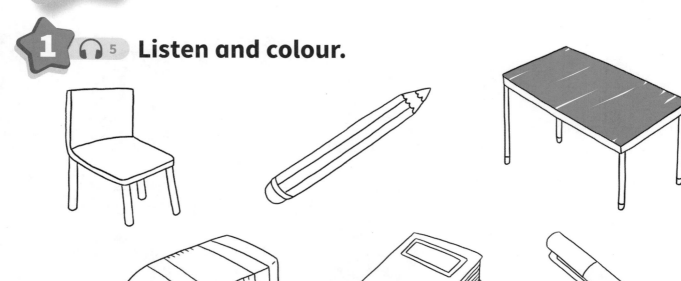

2 ★ **Draw your table. Say.**

> The table is blue. The book is red.

Me!

Me!

🔲 Do the online activities on Practice Extra as you complete this unit.

Draw three pictures.

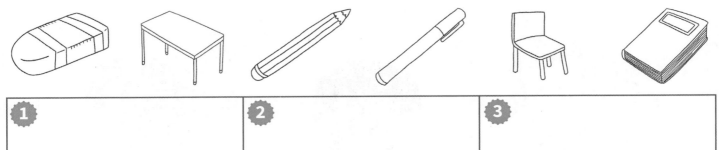

1	2	3

**Tell your friend.
Draw your friend's pictures.**

Number one is a chair.

1	2	3

 Count and write the number. Say.

Tables.　Four!

 4　　　

 **6 Listen and write the number.**

⭐ **2 Follow the lines and say.**

6 8 5 9 7

Language: question words *How old is he/she? He's/She's (nine).*

Starters Reading and Writing

1 Look and read. Put a tick (✓) or a cross (✗) in the box .

Example

This is a pencil. ✗

1

This is a book. ☐

2

This is a table. ☐

3

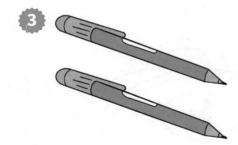

These are erasers. ☐

4

This is a bag. ☐

1 **Read and match.**

book

bag

pencil

pen

2 **Look and draw.**

My picture dictionary

1 Find and stick.

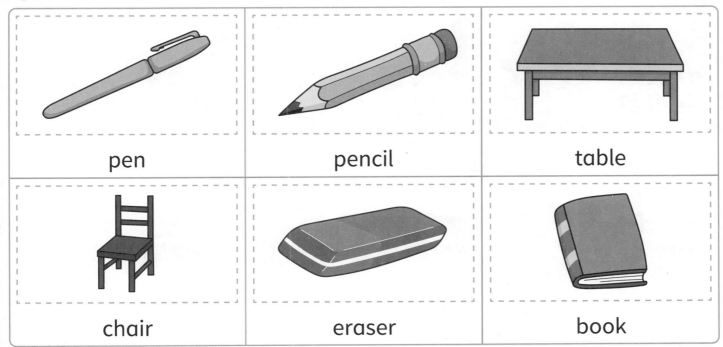

pen	pencil	table
chair	eraser	book

My star card

2 Say the words. Colour the stars.

Marie's art

What happens when you mix colours?

1 🎧 7 **Listen and colour. Say.**

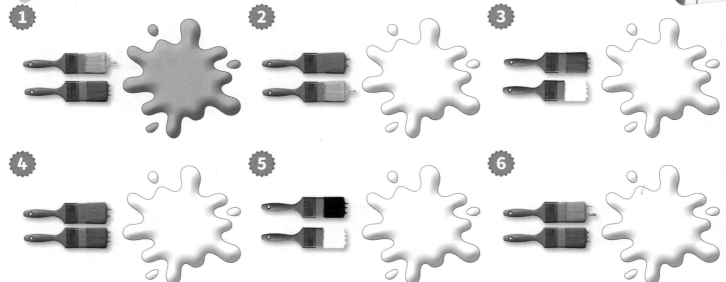

2 **Look and write. Circle the pictures of primary colours.**

red   blue   yellow

_____

pink

purple

_____

orange

green

3 Now you! **Play and say.**

This is a purple pencil.

Art: mix colours | 🧠 critical thinking

Trevor's values

Make friends

 Draw and colour two friends. Ask, answer and write.

What's your name?　　How old are you?

I'm ___Sam___ .
I'm ___seven___ .

I'm _____ .
I'm _____ .

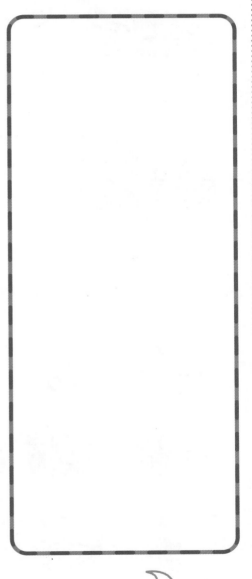

I'm _____ .
I'm _____ .

3 Favourite toys

1 🎧 8 Listen and circle the tick or cross.

1. ✓ ✗
2. ✓ ✗
3. ✓ ✗
4. ✓ ✗
5. ✓ ✗
6. ✓ ✗

2 Look and match. Say.

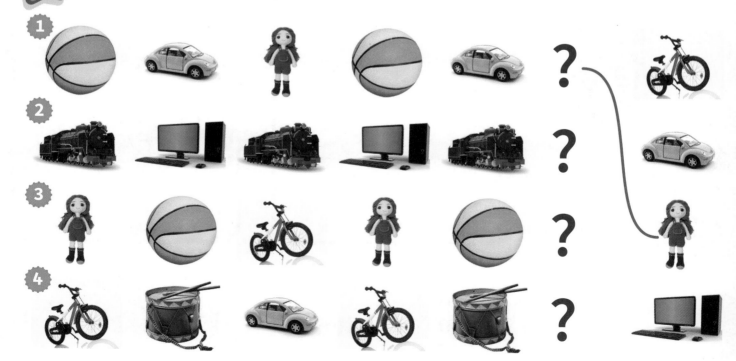

1. ?
2. ?
3. ?
4. ?

Vocabulary: toys ▶ Do the online activities on **Practice Extra** as you complete this unit.

 🎧 9 **Listen and draw coloured lines.**

2 **Colour the toys.**

Now ask and answer. Colour your friend's toys.

What colour's your ball? It's green.

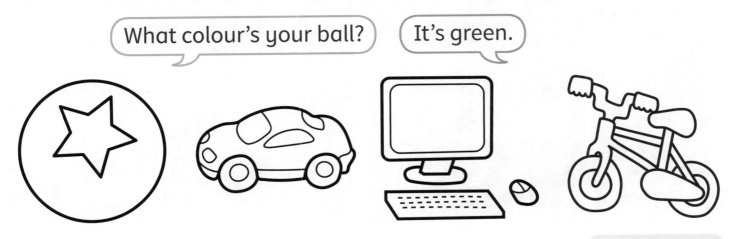

 **1** 🎧 10 **Listen and write the number.**

1

 2 **Find and circle the differences.**

Language: prepositions of place *It's in / on / under / next to the (train).*

1 🎧 11 🐵 **Listen and draw lines.**

Matt   Alice   Hugo

Eva   Mark   Mary

Monty's sounds and spelling

1 🎧 12 **Listen and circle 't' or 'd'.**

① t d

② t d

③ t d

④ t d

⑤ t d

⑥ t d

⑦ t d

⑧ t d

2 **Look and write 't' or 'd'.**

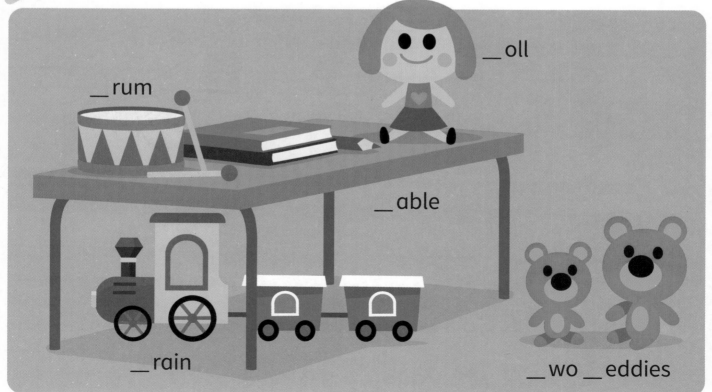

__oll

__rum

__able

__rain

__wo __eddies

My picture dictionary

1 Find and stick.

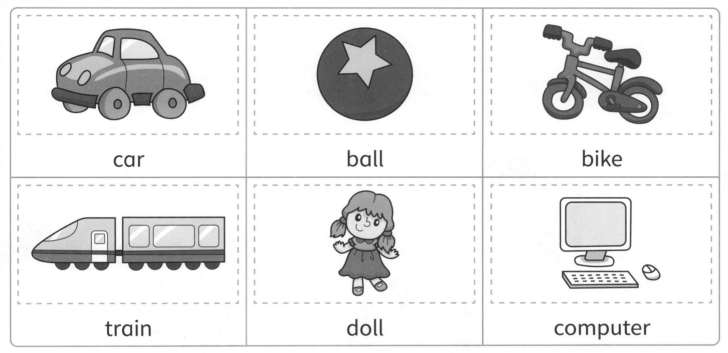

car	ball	bike
train	doll	computer

My star card

2 Say the words. Colour the stars.

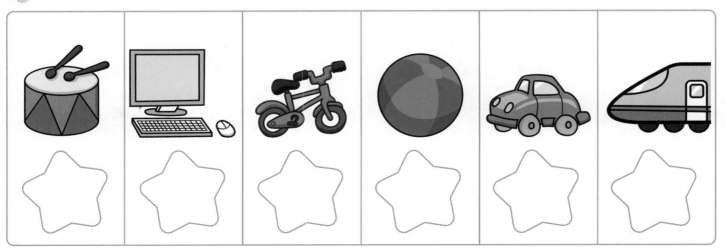

4 my family

1 Look and write the number. Say.

Number 1!

Stella. His sister.

1 Stella	2 Mr Star	3 Grandpa Star
4 Mrs Star	5 Suzy	6 Grandma Star

 1

2 🎧 13 Listen and colour.

This is my family.

24
Vocabulary: family 　 Do the online activities on Practice Extra as you complete this unit.

1 🎧 14 Listen and draw coloured lines.

2 Draw your family. Say.

He's my brother.

Me!

Vocabulary: family   25

1 🎧 15 **Listen and colour the stars.**

This is my family.

 2 **Look and circle. Say and guess.**

Happy. Happy. Sad. Happy.

Number 1.

 1

 2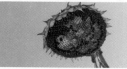

 3

 4

 5

Language: adjectives *She's (young).*

Starters Reading and Writing

1  **Look and complete the words.**

Example

 b e a u t i f u l

f t b a i
u e l u

1

_ _ _ _ _ _

o   d   l

2

_ _ _ _

d   s   a

3

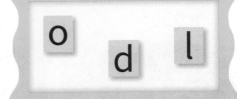

_ _ _ _ _

u   y
l   g

4

p   h   y
p   a

5

u   y   g
n   o

monty's sounds and spelling

1 🎧 16 **Listen and circle the 'a' in the words.**

c@t

sad

bag

happy

family

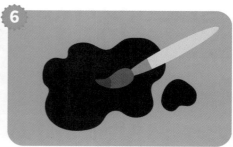

black

2 **Look and match.**

hat

dad

happy

cat

black

My picture dictionary

1 Find and stick.

grandfather

grandmother

mother

father

brother

sister

 # My star card

2 Say the words. Colour the stars.

Marie's science

Which planets are near Earth?

 Look, read and tick.

This is the planet where we live.

Earth ✓
Jupiter ☐

This planet is called 'the red planet'.

Venus ☐
Mars ☐

This planet is very big.

Mercury ☐
Jupiter ☐

This planet is next to the Sun.

Mercury ☐
Earth ☐

2 **Look and write.** Jupiter   Earth   the Sun

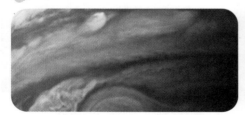  

_____   _____   _____

3 Now you! **Play and say.**   I'm a red planet.   You're Mars!

Trevor's values

Be kind

 Look, read and write the number.

Here you are.

OK!

Let's tidy up!

That's OK.

I'm sorry.

Thank you!

1

1 🎧 17 Listen and join the dots.

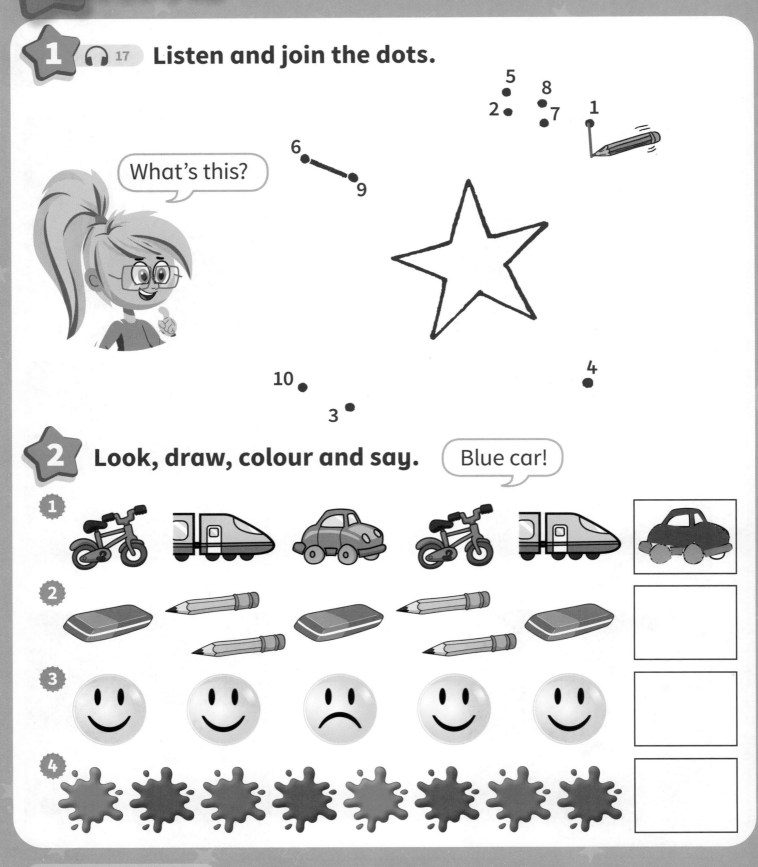

What's this?

2 Look, draw, colour and say.

Blue car!

3 ⭐ Say, look and answer.

Purple, one.   He's young!   Green, three.   It's a car!

1   **2**   **3**   **4**   **5**

5 Our pets

1 🎧 18 Listen and circle the tick or cross.

 1 ✓ ✗

 2 ✓ ✗

 3 ✓ ✗

 4 ✓ ✗

 5 ✓ ✗

 6 ✓ ✗

2 Look and write.

a bird   a cat   a dog   a fish   a horse   ~~a mouse~~

 1

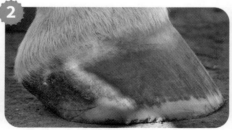 2

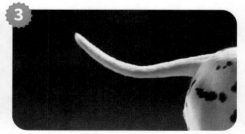 3

a mouse

 4

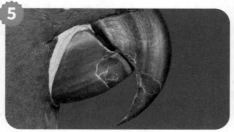 5

 6

Vocabulary: animals   ▶ Do the online activities on Practice Extra as you complete this unit.

Colour the pets.

Now ask and answer. Colour your friend's pets.

What colour is the fish?   It's blue.

 Read and write the answer.

birds   ~~fish~~   mice   cats   horses

1 What are they?
They're ____fish____ .

2 What are they?
They're _____ .

3 What are they?
They're _____ .

4 What are they?
They're _____ .

5 What are they?
They're _____ .

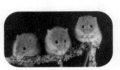

Look, read and circle.

1

short / (long)

2

clean / dirty

3

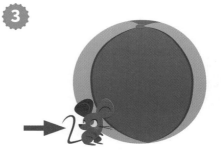

small / big

4

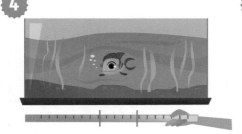

short / long

5

big / small

6

clean / dirty

 🎧 19 **Listen and follow.**

Language presentation: adjectives *They're (clean).*

Starters Reading and Writing

1  **Look and read. Put a tick (✓) or a cross (✗) in the box.**

Example

This is a horse.　

1

These are birds.　

2

This is a mouse.　

3

This is a cat.　

4

This is a fish.

monty's sounds and spelling

 1 Draw lines to make two words.

r   e

p   e   d   t

 2 Look and write.

My r____ p____.

3 🎧 20 **Listen and write 'a' or 'e'.**

1 p_e_ts   2 b__g   3 c__t   4 p__n

5 t_n   6 s_d   7 St_lla   8 h_ppy

My picture dictionary

1 **Find and stick.**

dog	bird	cat
fish	mouse	horse

My star card

2 **Say the words. Colour the stars.**

6 My face

1 🎧 21 **Listen and draw coloured lines.**

① ② ③ ④ ⑤ ⑥

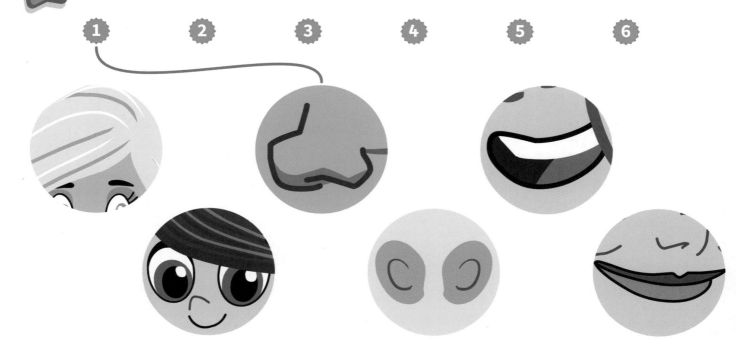

2 **Circle the different word.**

1	(table)	horse	mouse	bird
2	bike	nose	train	doll
3	eyes	ears	teeth	ball
4	book	pen	car	pencil
5	fish	horse	cat	head
6	dog	four	ten	seven

 **22** **Listen and write the number.**

 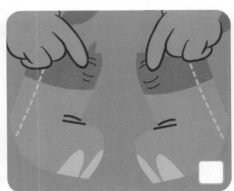 

 Look and write.

e a r s   e y e s   n o s e   m o u t h

t e e t h   h a i r

e a r s

Vocabulary: the body and face   41

 **🎧 23 Listen and draw. Listen and colour.**

2 Draw your face and write.

Me!

blue
brown
green
big
small
short
long

I've got _____ eyes.
I've got a _____ mouth.
I've got _____ hair.

Language: have got for possession *I've got (a small mouth).*

Starters Reading and Writing

1  **Read and write.**

A monster

I'm a happy monster. My ___head___ is very big. I've got long pink
(1) _____ . I've got three (2) _____ . On my
face, my (3) _____ is small, but I haven't got a small
mouth. In my mouth, I've got big (4) _____ .
I've got a pet. My pet is a (5) _____ .

Example

head

teeth

ears

cat

hair

nose

Monty's sounds and spelling

 Look and write.

t̲wo ears

_wo

eyes

__ree

_ee___

mou___

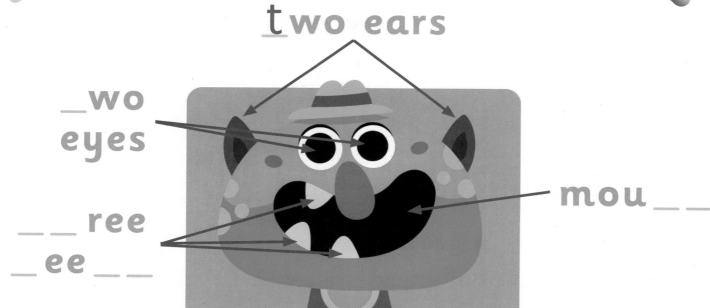

 Read and draw.

I'm Mrs Monster.
I've got three teeth.

I'm Mr Monster.
I've got one tooth.

My picture dictionary

1 Find and stick.

? ? ? ?	? ? ? ?	? ? ? ?
ears	eyes	mouth
? ? ? ?	? ? ? ?	? ? ? ?
nose	hair	teeth

My star card

2 Say the words. Colour the stars.

Marie's science

How do we use our senses?

1 🎧 24 **Listen and write the number. Look and circle.**

The rabbit has got big ears / hands.

The fish has got big ears / eyes.

1

His (nose) / hand is in the flowers.

The horse has got big hands / teeth.

The girl feels the cat with her hand / eye.

2 **Follow and write the words. Say.**

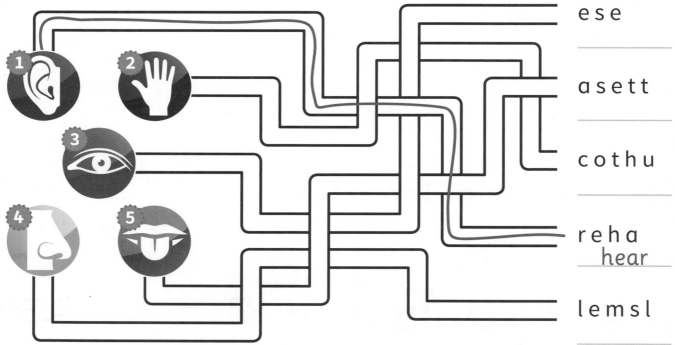

e s e

a s e t t

c o t h u

r e h a
hear

l e m s l

3 Now you! **Ask and answer.**

What can you hear?   I can hear birds.

Science: the senses | 🎓 learning to learn

Trevor's values

Look after pets

** Look, read and match.**

1

2

I brush my cat.

I wash my horse.

I feed my fish.

I walk my dog.

3

4

2 Draw and write.

Me!

This is my _____ . I _____ and _____ my _____ .

7 ★ Wild animals

1 🎧 25 Listen and join the dots.

2 Find and circle the words.

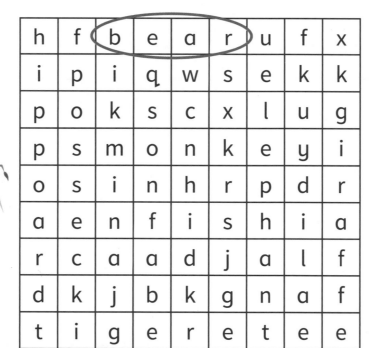

h	f	b	e	a	r	u	f	x
i	p	i	q	w	s	e	k	k
p	o	k	s	c	x	l	u	g
p	s	m	o	n	k	e	y	i
o	s	i	n	h	r	p	d	r
a	e	n	f	i	s	h	i	a
r	c	a	a	d	j	a	l	f
d	k	j	b	k	g	n	a	f
t	i	g	e	r	e	t	e	e

Vocabulary: animals   ▶ Do the online activities on **Practice Extra** as you complete this unit.

Read, look and write 'yes' or 'no'.

1 Are the giraffes sad? _no_

2 Are the elephants happy? _____

3 Are the crocodiles long? _____

4 Are the snakes short? _____

5 Are the bears dirty? _____

 Colour the animals.

Now say. Colour your friend's animals.

My giraffes are purple.

 **1** 🎧 26 **Listen and write the number. Colour.**

[ ] (hippos)   [ ] (snakes)

[ ] (giraffes)   [1] (elephants)

[ ] (lions)   [ ] (crocodiles)

2 **Look and cross or tick .**

Animals	hands	arms	legs	feet	tails
snakes	✗	✗	✗	✗	✓
bears					
birds					
monkeys					
crocodiles					
fish					
tigers					
giraffes					

Language: have got for possession *They've got (tails). They haven't got (legs).*

Starters Reading and Writing

1 **Look and read. Write 'yes' or 'no'.**

Example

The elephants have got small ears.   _no_

1   The monkeys are on bikes.   _____

2   The giraffes are under the elephants.   _____

3   The tigers have got red noses.   _____

4   The crocodiles are next to the tigers.   _____

5   The snakes have got green eyes.   _____

monty's sounds and spelling

1 **Read, match and say.**

Six king elephants.

Ten little hippos.

2 🎧 27 **Listen and write 'a', 'e' or 'i'.**

1 l e g

2 f __ sh

3 bl __ ck

4 b __ g

5 h __ ppo

6 p __ n

7 s __ ster

8 h __ nd

3 **Read and draw.**

Little king elephant.

My picture dictionary

1 **Find and stick.**

crocodile	elephant	tiger
hippo	giraffe	snake

My star card

2 **Say the words. Colour the stars.**

8 My clothes

1 Look, find and circle the number. Say.

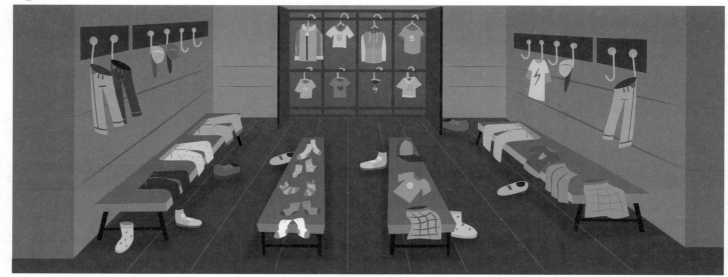

Seven pairs of trousers.

trousers	1	2	3	4	5	6	⑦	8	9	10
socks	1	2	3	4	5	6	7	8	9	10
T-shirts	1	2	3	4	5	6	7	8	9	10
skirts	1	2	3	4	5	6	7	8	9	10
shoes	1	2	3	4	5	6	7	8	9	10
jackets	1	2	3	4	5	6	7	8	9	10
caps	1	2	3	4	5	6	7	8	9	10

2 🎧 28 Listen and answer.

Jackets? Two!

Vocabulary: clothes 📱 Do the online activities on Practice Extra as you complete this unit.

1  🎧 29 Listen and colour.

2 Draw and write.

Me!

My favourite clothes are my _____ .

 **1** 🎧 30 **Listen and colour.**

2 🎧 31 **Listen and match.**

Vocabulary: clothes | **Language:** have got for possession *He's/She's got (a black shoe).*

Starters Listening

1 🎧 32 **Read the question. Listen and write a name or a number. There are two examples.**

3   ~~Kim~~   Tom   ~~10~~   8   Bill   9

Examples

What is the girl's name?	Kim
How old is she?	10

1 What is the dog's name? _____

2 How old is the dog? _____

3 What is the name of Kim's brother? _____

4 How old is Kim's brother? _____

5 How many children are in Kim's class? _____

monty's sounds and spelling

1 **Write 's' or 'sh' and match.**

1 __kirt   **2** T-__irt

3 __ocks   **4** __oes

2 **Read and draw.**

| A crocodile in a red skirt and green socks. | A dog in purple shorts and orange shoes. |

3 **Write the sentences.**

1

an orange   She's got   skirt.

She's got an orange skirt.

2

socks.   six blue   He's got

3

They've got   shorts.   white

My picture dictionary

1 **Find and stick.**

jacket	shoes	skirt
socks	trousers	T-shirt

 My star card

2 **Say the words. Colour the stars.**

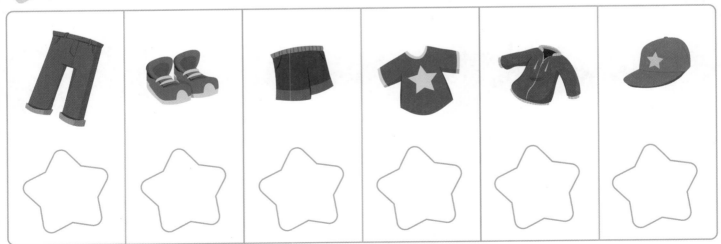

marie's geography

Where do animals live?

1 Look and write 'g' for garden, 'p' for polar region and 's' for savannah.

 g  p  s

     p

2 🎧 33 **Listen and circle.**

Habitat: forest / savannah
Animals: lion / polar bear
Climate: hot / cold

Habitat: polar region / garden
Animals: penguin / tiger
Climate: hot / cold

Habitat: forest / garden
Animals: fox / zebra

3 Now you! **Write, draw and say.**

In _____ (country) there is
a _____ (habitat) region. There are
_____ and _____ (animals).

Trevor's values

Love nature

 Read and write the number.

We can use less water. [3]   We can plant a tree. ☐
Recycling is fun! ☐   We can keep parks clean. ☐

 Draw and write.

I love nature!

I _____ to help nature.

1 **Read, draw and colour.**

Ben

Bill

Bill
~~short shoes~~
a dirty T-shirt
a big nose
a sad mouth
a red jacket
long black hair

Ben
big shoes
a happy mouth
green hair
a small nose
purple trousers
short red hair

2 🎧 34 **Listen and say 'Bill' or 'Ben'.**

3 **Say the sentences.**  Fish and snakes haven't got legs.

 and  no legs.

 and 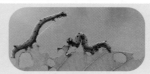 no hands.

 and  no arms.

 and  no hair.

4 **Look, read and write.**

arms   ears   ~~face~~   hands   mouth   tail   two   two

At the safari park

I'm small and brown. I've got a funny ① ___face___

2

with ② _____ big ③ _____ and a big ④ _____ .

My ⑤ _____ are long and

2

I've got ⑥ _____

big ⑦ _____ . I've got

a long ⑧ _____ .

9 Fun time!

1 🎧 35 Listen and write the number.

2 Look and match.

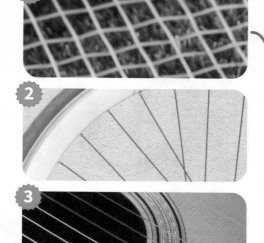

swim

play the guitar

play tennis

ride a bike

play football

play basketball

Vocabulary: sports and leisure   ▶ Do the online activities on **Practice Extra** as you complete this unit.

Find and circle six words.

w	a	s	g	r	i	d	e
r	s	p	u	g	i	t	a
a	w	b	i	k	e	r	p
t	i	n	t	i	s	l	l
o	m	l	a	s	t	c	a
o	m	e	r	x	u	r	y
t	e	n	n	i	s	a	e

? a ?

? ?

?

play the ?

 Look and write.

football ~~guitar~~ play ride swim tennis

1 play the ___guitar___
2 _____ basketball
3 play _____

4 play _____
5 _____ a bike
6 _____

1 🎧 36 Listen and tick or cross.

 X

 6

2 What can you do? Draw and write.

Me!

✓	X
✓	X

I can _____

_____

_____ .

I can't _____

_____

_____ .

Language: can for ability *I/You can (play tennis). He/She can't (swim).*

Starters Reading and Writing

1 Look and write the words.

Example

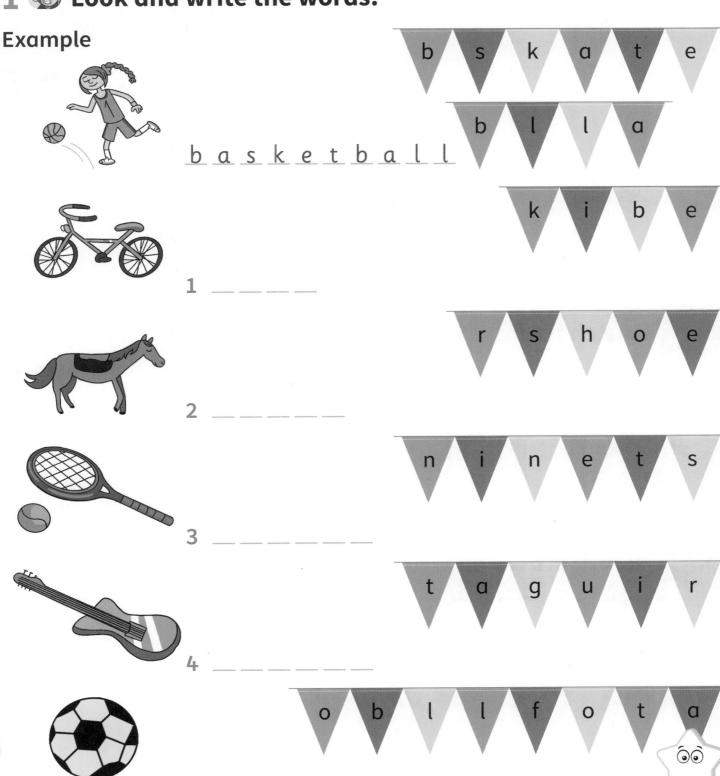

b s k a t e

b a s k e t b a l l

b l l a

k i b e

1 _ _ _ _ _

r s h o e

2 _ _ _ _ _

n i n e t s

3 _ _ _ _ _

t a g u i r

4 _ _ _ _ _ _

o b l l f o t a

5 _ _ _ _ _ _ _ _

monty's sounds and spelling

 1 **Look and write. Complete the table.**

snail	day	play
train	~~say~~	tail

s a y _____ _____

ay	ai
say	tail

_____ _____ _____

 2 **Match to make sentences. Say and write.**

We can play tennis.

We can	play	a bike.
I can't	play	the piano.
We can't	play	tennis.
They can	ride	a game.

 3 **Read, draw and write the answer.**

What can you play on a grey day?

_____

_____

My picture dictionary

1 Find and stick.

play basketball	ride a bike	play tennis
swim	play football	play the guitar

My star card

2 Say the words. Colour the stars.

10 At the funfair

1 Look and write.

bike   boat   bus   car   ~~helicopter~~
lorry   motorbike   plane   train

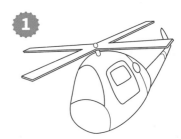

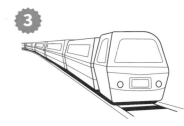

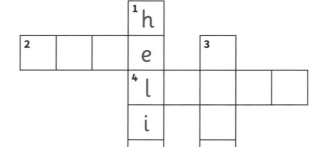

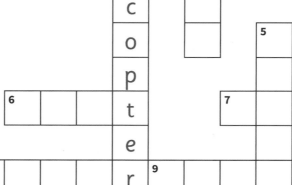

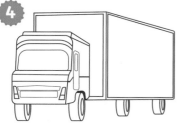

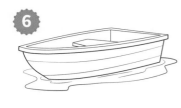

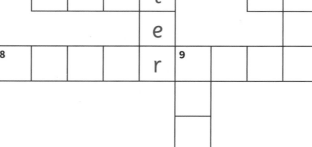

Crossword:

1 (down) h e l i c o p t e r

2 🎧 37 Listen and colour.

▷ Do the online activities on Practice Extra as you complete this unit.

Draw stars in, on, under or next to the pictures.

Now ask and answer. Draw your friend's stars.

Where's the star?

It's under the bus.

 Look and write.

lorry   T-shirt   helicopter   boat   trousers   plane
skirt   jacket   cap   motorbike   shorts   bus

lorry

T-shirt

 **1** 🎧 38 **Listen and draw coloured lines.**

 2 **Draw and write. Say.**

> I'm riding a horse.

riding   horse   bike   motorbike   driving
lorry   bus   boat   flying   plane   helicopter

Me!

I'm _____ a _____ .

Language: present continuous (not with future reference) *What are you doing? I'm (riding a horse).*

Starters Listening

1 🎧 39 🐵 **Listen and tick (✓) the box. There is one example.**

Where is the lorry?

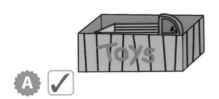 **A** ✓

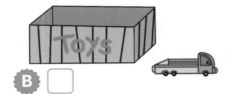 **B** ☐

 **C** ☐

1 What is Anna doing?

 **A** ☐

 **B** ☐

 **C** ☐

2 What toy is under the chair?

 **A** ☐

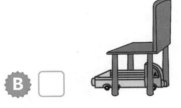 **B** ☐

 **C** ☐

3 What colour is Matt's motorbike?

 **A** ☐

 **B** ☐

 **C** ☐

4 Which boy is Alex?

 **A** ☐

 **B** ☐

 **C** ☐

monty's sounds and spelling

 1 Read and circle 'ng'. Choose and draw.

1 I'm flyi(ng) my plane.

2 I'm singing a song.

3 I'm riding my motorbike.

4 I'm clapping my hands.

 2 Look and write.

clapping ~~singing~~	my hands a helicopter
flying	~~a song~~

I'm singing a song.

_____

_____

 3 Read and write.

flying   ~~driving~~   riding   flying   driving   riding

1 I'm ____driving____ a lorry.

2 I'm _____ a plane.

3 You're _____
a motorbike.

4 You're _____ a car.

5 I'm _____ a horse.

6 You're _____
a helicopter.

My picture dictionary

1 **Find and stick.**

? ? ? ? ? bus	? ? ? ? ? lorry	? ? ? ? ? motorbike
? ? ? ? ? helicopter	? ? ? ? ? plane	? ? ? ? ? ship

My star card

2 **Say the words. Colour the stars.**

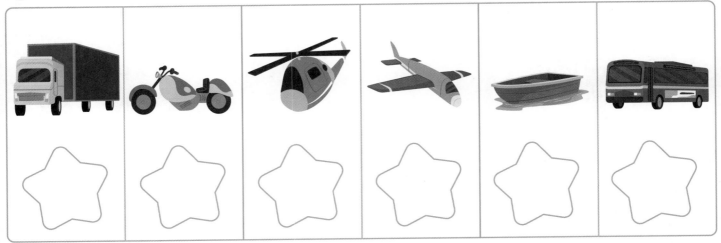

Marie's geography

How do we travel?

1 **Look and write the number.**

1 road   2 water   3 air   4 rail

3

2 **Read and match. Draw lines.**

1 A helicopter travels …   … on the road.
2 A ship travels …   … on the water.
3 A train travels …   … on rails.
4 A scooter travels …   … in the air.

3 Now you! **Now you! Ask and answer.**

It travels in the air.   A helicopter?   No!   A plane?   Yes!

Trevor's values

Work together

1 **Read and write the number.**

1 Give me your hand. I can help you.

2 Let's work together. We can do it.

3 Here's some water.

4 We're a team – let's go!

11 Our house

Alex   Dan   Grace   Hugo

May   Bill   Sue

1 Follow the lines and write.

bedroom   ~~living room~~   kitchen   hall

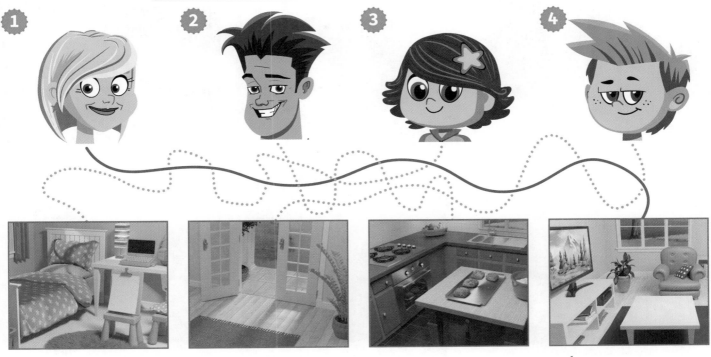

living room

---

2 Draw your house. Write and say.

Me!

My house has got

_____

_____

_____

_____

_____

_____

1 🎧 41 Listen and colour the stars.

2 Match and write.

1 She's drawing a ___picture___ .

2 He's reading a _____ .

3 She's sitting on a _____ .

4 They're listening to _____ .

5 He's driving a _____ .

6 They're playing a _____ .

 chair

 videogame

 car

 book

 music

 picture

Language: present continuous *What's he/she doing? He's/She's (driving a car).*

Starters Reading and Writing

1 🐵 Look, read and write. Use one word.

Examples

Where are the children?	in the _____ kitchen
How many people are there?	_____ two
1 What's the girl eating?	some _____
2 What's the boy got?	a _____

3 What's the girl doing?	listening to _____
4 What animals can the boy see?	_____

5 Who is pointing?	the _____

monty's sounds and spelling

1 Read and write. Look and circle 'yes' or 'no'.

1 The monkey's watching TV in the bedroo__ .

2 The __ouse's riding a bike in the dining roo__ .

3 Grand__a's singing in the hall.

4 A horse's cooking in the kitchen.

yes / no

yes / no

yes / no

yes / no

2 Choose and write. Draw and write.

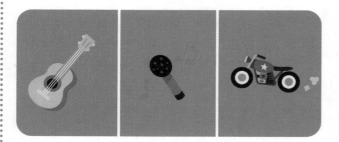

| monkey mouse hippo singing |
| riding a motorbike playing the guitar |
| bedroom living room dining room |

The monkey's riding a motorbike in the dining room.

My picture dictionary

1 **Find and stick.**

living room	bedroom	kitchen
bathroom	hall	dining room

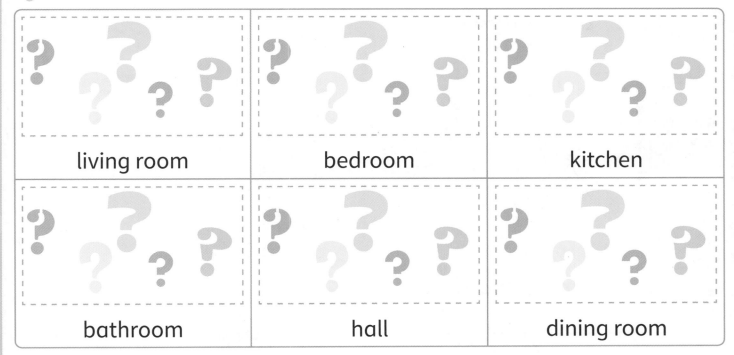

My star card

2 **Say the words. Colour the stars.**

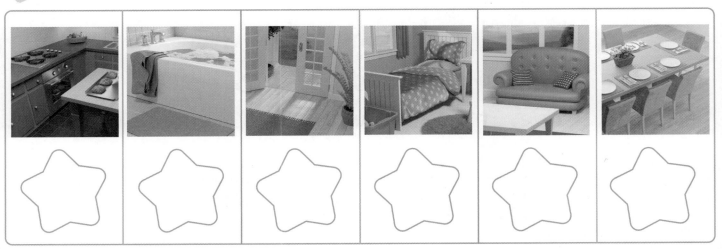

12 Party time!

2 **Find, circle and write.**

a	w	e	i	f	i	s	h	s
c	h	o	c	o	l	a	t	e
a	b	r	e	c	k	f	a	m
k	l	t	c	h	e	j	p	r
e	b	u	r	g	e	r	p	o
p	r	o	e	v	i	s	l	b
b	a	n	a	n	a	t	e	g
j	z	o	m	e	r	s	t	u
o	r	a	n	g	e	v	i	e

1   apple

5 _____

2 _____

6 _____

3 _____

7 _____

4 _____

8 _____

1 Look and write.

1. → _____cat_____

2. → _____

3. → _____

4. → _____

2 Read and write.

young
~~eating~~
banana
cake

The small monkey's ___eating___ an orange and the big monkey's got some _____. The old monkey's eating a _____ and the _____ monkey's got some ice cream.

85

 **Listen and tick or cross.**

1 ✓

2

3

4

 Look and write 'like' or 'don't like'.

Me!

I _____ fish.

Me!

I _____ burgers.

Me!

I _____ ice cream.

Me!

I _____ _____ .

Language: present simple: *I like (fish). I don't like (burgers).*

Starters Listening

1 🎧 44 🐵 **Listen and colour. There is one example.**

monty's sounds and spelling

1 ⭐ Look, write and match.

1 ● rainbow
2 ● book
3 ● pencil
4 ● doll
5 ● train
6 ● hat
7 ● teeth
8 ● hippo
9 ● elephant
10 ● shoe
11 ● sock
12 ● mouse
13 ● riding

tr a i n [5]	__ ock [ ]
__ ainbow [ ]	__ lephan __ [ ]
__ oll [ ]	__ oe [ ]
h __ __ __ [ ]	h __ ppo [ ]
__ ouse [ ]	si __ [ ]
__ ook [ ]	__ encil [ ]
tee __ __ __ [ ]	

2 ⭐ Think and write. Then draw.

1 The _____ and the _____ are playing the piano.

2 My pet _____ likes to wear _____ .

3 On the train there's a green _____ , a purple _____ and a beautiful _____ .

3 ⭐ Look and circle the words. Say.

mousehipporainbowpenbookridingredhappyteethtrain

Sounds and spelling review: r / b / p / d / t / a / e / th / i / sh / s / ng / m / ai

My picture dictionary

1 Find and stick.

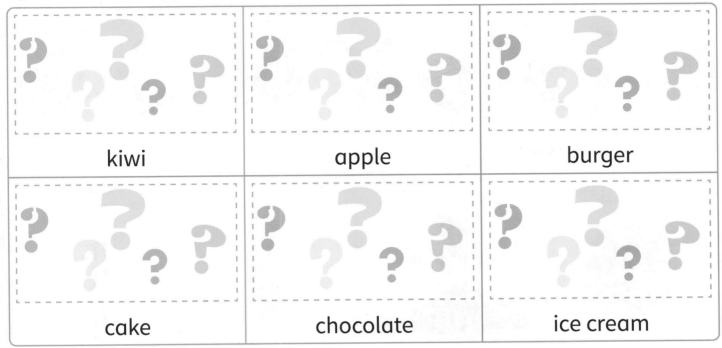

kiwi	apple	burger
cake	chocolate	ice cream

My star card

2 Say the words. Colour the stars.

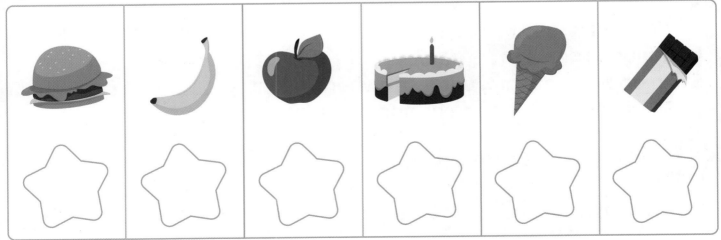

Marie's science

How does fruit grow?

1 **Look and match. Say.**

1 2 3 4 5 6 7

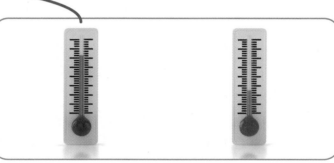

2 **Read and write.**

| the ground | trees | big | ~~hot~~ | small | strawberries |

1 Oranges grow in _____hot_____ places.
2 _____ grow on plants in cold places.
3 Watermelons are very _____ and grow on the ground.
4 Bananas grow on _____ in hot places.
5 An apple tree is big, but a strawberry plant is _____ .
6 Some fruit grows on trees and some grows near _____ .

3 **Now you!** **Ask and answer.**

Watermelons?

They grow on the ground in hot countries.

Trevor's values

Keep clean

Number the pictures in order.

A: 2 | 3 | 1

B

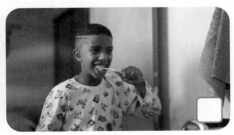

C

Look, read and write.

teeth   apples   hands

1 He's washing his

2 She's brushing her

3 She's washing her

_____.

_____.

_____.

1 **Tick one box for each monster.**

reading a book						
eating fish						
watching TV						
having a bath						

Now ask and answer. Tick your friend's boxes.

What's the old monster doing?   He's eating fish.

reading a book						
eating fish						
watching TV						
having a bath						

Circle the different word. Say.

1 kiwi   apple   orange   (guitar)
2 lorry   ice cream   train   bus
3 burger   tiger   giraffe   lion
4 bathroom   kitchen   bedroom   chocolate
5 motorbike   helicopter   hall   lorry
6 play   swim   bike   ride

 Read and write. Draw.

Me!

I'm _____ .
I'm at home in the kitchen. I like _____ , but I don't like _____ .
My favourite food is _____ .

Grammar reference

 1 Order the questions. Write the number.

1 (your) ☐   (name?) ☐   (What's) ☐

2 (old) ☐   (are) ☐   (you?) ☐   (How) ☐

2 Read and circle.

1 He's / She's Simon.   He's / She's six.

2 He's / She's Stella.   He's / She's seven.

3 Read and write.

(isn't   Is   Is   is)

1 _____ your ball in your car?   Yes, it _____.

2 _____ your ball on the table?   No, it _____.

 4 Circle the sentences.

We aren't sad. We're happy. Are we beautiful?

5 **Read and write.**

They're   It's

1 Look at the dog. _____ long.
2 Look at the two cats. _____ small.

 6 **Order the words. Write the sentences.**

1 (face.) (got) (I've) (a clean) _____
2 (You've) (short) (hair.) (got) _____

 7 **Circle the sentences.**

They'vegottails.Theyhaven'tgothair.Havetheygotlegs?

8 **Read and write.**

hasn't got   's got

1 ✓ He _____ your red trousers.
2 ✗ He _____ your blue hat.

Order the words. Write the sentences.

1 (can) (sing.) (He) _____

2 (swim.) (They) (can't) _____

3 (ride) (Can) (you) (a bike?) _____

 Read and write.

(am   Are   not   Are)

1 _____ you flying a plane?   Yes, I _____ .

2 _____ you playing the guitar?   No, I'm _____ .

 Circle the sentences.

What'shedoing?He'shavingabath.Ishereading.?

 Read and write.

(like   don't like   don't like   like)

1 ☺ I _____ cake.

2 ☹ I _____ ice cream.

3 ☹ I _____ fish.

4 ☺ I _____ apples.